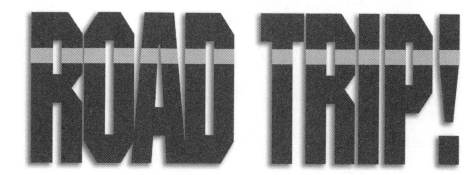

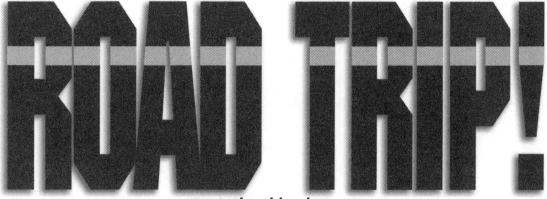

ROAD TRIP!

Zits® Sketchbook No. 7

by JERRY SCOTT and JIMBORGMAN"

Andrews McMeel
Publishing

Kansas City

To Andrew and Erin, Domers united.

—J.S.

With thanks and more thanks to my big-hearted friends,
Sandi, Steve, Misha, and Maya.

—J.B

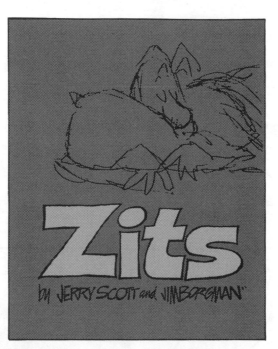

15

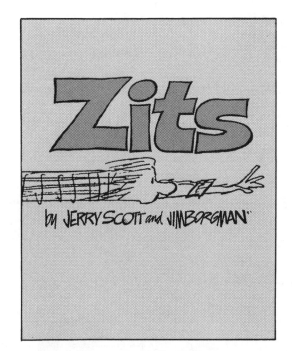

21

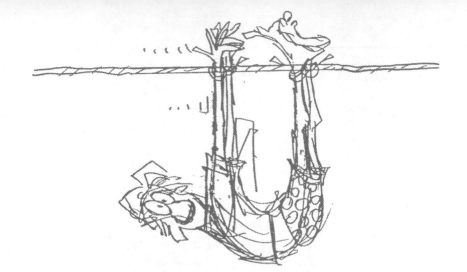

24

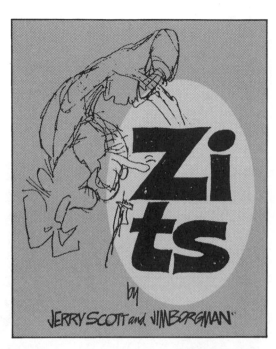

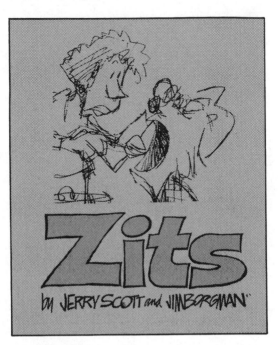

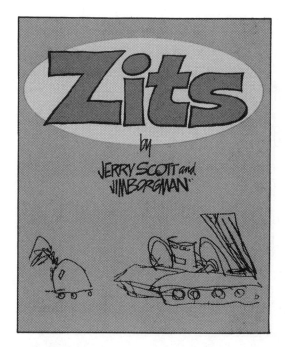

63

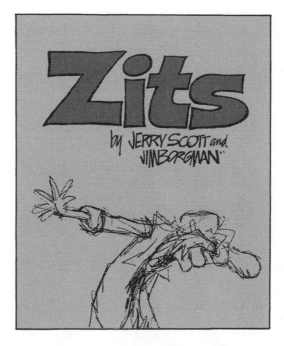

'MORNING, JEREMY

'NITE, DAD

SEE YOU WHEN I GET HOME FROM WORK

IF I'M UP BY THEN

YAWN!

SCOTT and BORGMAN

HOW CAN TWO PEOPLE BE LIVING IN OPPOSITE TIME ZONES IN THE SAME HOUSE?

GOOD MORNING, SUNSHINE!

PANCAKES?

SCOTT and BORGMAN

READ THIS COMIC STRIP!

IT'S SO YOUR DAD!

"...SO IT TURNS OUT THAT I HAD BEEN WEARING GRANDMA'S GLASSES THE WHOLE TIME!

IS THAT A SCREAM?

STILL TRYING TO GET YOUR SON TO SHOW SOME EMOTION, HUH?

IT'S LIKE COAXING A SMILE OUT OF A CLAM FULL OF BOTOX.

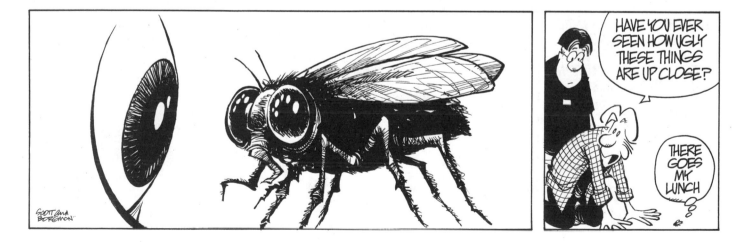

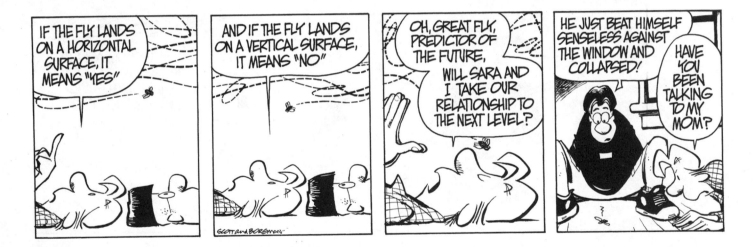

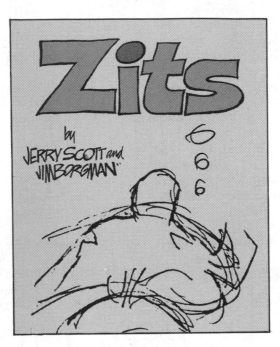

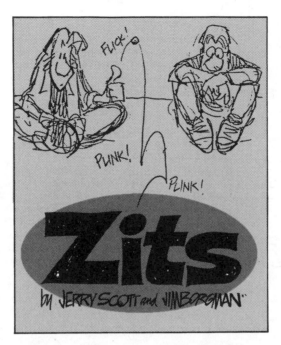

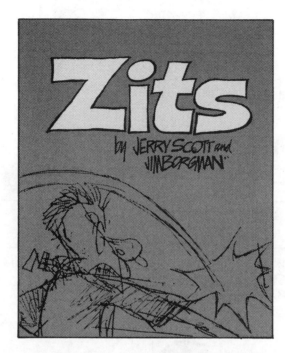

Surgeon General's Warning: Laboratory tests have shown that forcing the corners of one's mouth to lift in a contrived or insincere manner before noon may be hazardous to your health.

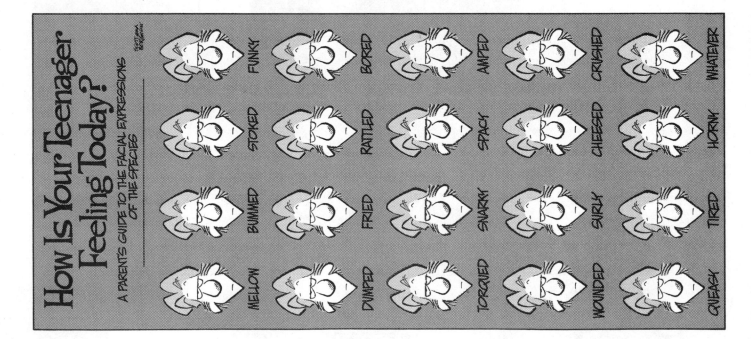

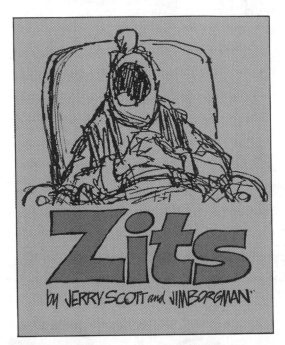

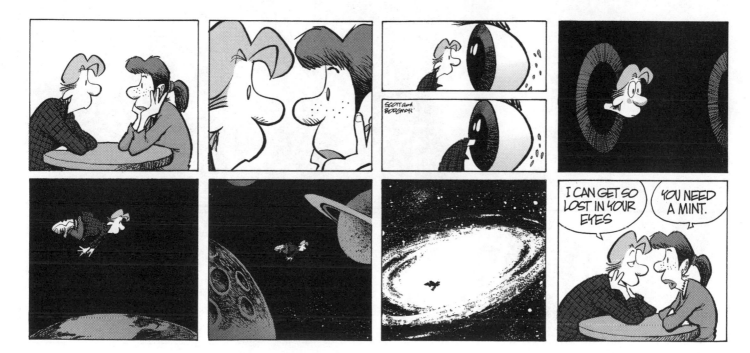

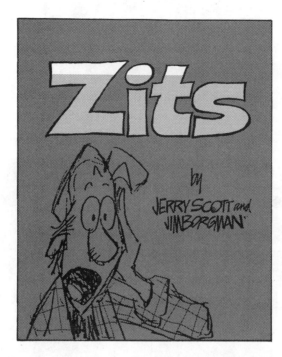

Zits

by JERRY SCOTT and JIM BORGMAN

OOOOOH

MY BRAIN HURTS!

POOR BABY, LET'S TAKE A LOOK.

WELL, NO WONDER!

LOOK AT THE MESS IN HERE!

ONCE IN AWHILE YOU HAVE TO CLEAN OUT ALL OF THE USELESS GARBAGE THAT'S JUST TAKING UP SPACE IN THERE.

THEN YOU CAN REORGANIZE AND PRIORITIZE YOUR IMPORTANT THOUGHTS IN A MUCH MORE EFFICIENT WAY.

FEEL BETTER?

YEAH!

GOOD. I'LL MAKE SOME COOKIES.

SOMETIMES MOM MAKES IT REALLY HARD FOR ME TO STAY SULLEN AND RESENTFUL.

I'LL PASS ALONG THE COMPLIMENT.